PUBLISHED BY NICHOLAS THOMPSON

Women Diet: Lose Weight, Improve Your Health

Published By Nicholas Thompson

@ Eric Dube

Women Diet: Lose Weight, Improve Your

Health

All Right RESERVED

ISBN 978-87-975002-9-3

TABLE OF CONTENTS

Moroccan Chickpea Stew 1

Thai Coconut Curry Soup 4

Grilled Chicken With Steamed Asparagus 6

Turkey Meatballs With Zucchini Noodles 8

Tofu And Vegetable Kebabs With A Side Of Couscous ... 11

Spinach And Mushroom Frittata With A Green Salad: ... 13

Almond And Coconut Energy Bites 16

Berry Greek Yogurt Parfait 18

Apple Cinnamon Quinoa Porridge 19

Baked Egg Cups 21

Breakfast Burritos 23

Salmon With Teriyaki Glaze And Brown Rice 25

Portobello Mushrooms Stuffed With Feta And Spinach 29

Grilled Chicken Wrap 31

Lentil Soup 33

- Buckwheat Pancakes With A Dollop Of Greek Yogurt And Sliced Almonds: 35
- Veggie And Cheese Wrap Using A Whole Grain Tortilla: 37
- Mediterranean Orange And Almond Cake 39
- Ayurvedic Greek Yogurt With Honey And Walnuts 42
- Ayurvedic Fig And Date Energy Balls 43
- Cauliflower Crust Pizza 45
- Spinach And Mushroom Omelet: 49
- Salad Of Black Beans And Quinoa With Avocado Dressing 51
- Grilled Chicken Breast With Greek Salad 53
- Lentil And Vegetable Stirfry 54
- Broccoli And Cauliflower Soup. 57
- Spinach And Mushroom Quiche 60
- Mexican Quinoa Skillet 63
- Mediterranean Lentil Soup 66
- Caprese Stuffed Portobello Mushrooms 69

Chicken Lettuce Wraps 71

Cauliflower Fried Rice 74

Black Bean And Sweet Potato Tacos With A Side Of Guacamole 77

Sautéed Shrimp With Zucchini Noodles And Pesto Sauce 79

Cauliflower Rice Stirfry With Tofu And Mixed Vegetables 81

Cinnamonroasted Chickpeas 83

Dark Chocolate Avocado Mousse 84

Spiced Pumpkin Seeds 85

Mediterranean Quinoa Bowl 86

Eggplant Lasagna 88

Chickpea Curry 91

Quinoa And Chickpea Salad 94

Tuna And Avocado Salad 96

Ayurvedic Pistachio Rosewater Cookies 97

Mediterranean Yogurt Parfait With Fresh Berries 100

Ayurvedic Date And Walnut Pudding 102

Shrimp And Vegetable Kebabs: 104

Black Bean And Sweet Potato Chili: 106

Caprese Salad With Grilled Chicken Or Sliced Turkey Breast: 109

Turkey And Vegetable Lettuce Wraps 111

Baked Sweet Potato With Black Bean Salsa 113

Veggie And Brown Rice Stir Fry 115

Roasted Beet And Goat Cheese Salad. 117

Mango And Avocado Salad. 119

Sesame Ginger Tofu Stir Fry. 121

Lemon Garlic Shrimp Stir Fry 123

Ginger Soy Chicken And Broccoli Stir Fry 126

Spicy Tofu And Mixed Vegetable Stir Fry 129

Pumpkin And Lentil Soup. 132

Cauliflower Rice And Veggie Stirfry.............................. 134

Asparagus Frittata 136

Moroccan Chickpea Stew

Ingredients:

- 1/2 tsp ground turmeric
- 1/2 tsp ground cinnamon
- 1/4 tsp cayenne pepper (optional, adjust to taste)
- 2 carrots, diced
- 1 red bell pepper, diced
- 1 can (14 ounces) diced tomatoes
- 2 cups cooked chickpeas
- 2 cups vegetable broth
- 1 tbsp olive oil

- 1 onion, diced
- 3 cloves garlic, minced
- 1 tsp ground cumin
- 1 tsp ground coriander
- Salt and pepper to taste
- Fresh cilantro, chopped (for garnish)

Directions:

1. Heat olive oil in a large pot over medium heat. Add the onion and garlic, and sauté until softened.
2. Stir in the cumin, coriander, turmeric, cinnamon, and cayenne pepper. Cook for 1 minute to release the flavors.
3. Add the carrots and red bell pepper to the pot and cook for 5 minutes, until slightly tender.
4. Pour in the diced tomatoes, cooked chickpeas, and vegetable broth. Bring to a boil, then reduce heat and simmer for 25 minutes.
5. Season with salt and pepper to taste. Serve the stew hot, garnished with fresh cilantro.

Thai Coconut Curry Soup

Ingredients:

- 3 cups vegetable broth
- 1 sweet potato, peeled and diced
- 1 cup broccoli florets
- 1 cup sliced mushrooms
- 1 red bell pepper, sliced
- 1 cup baby spinach
- 1 tbsp soy sauce (glutenfree if desired)
- Juice of 1 lime
- 1 tbsp coconut oil

- 1 onion, chopped
- 3 cloves garlic, minced
- 2 tbsps Thai red curry paste
- 1 can (14 ounces) coconut milk
- Fresh cilantro, chopped (for garnish)

Directions:

1. Heat coconut oil in a large pot over medium heat. Add the onion and garlic, and sauté until fragrant and softened.
2. Stir in the Thai red curry paste and cook for 1 minute to release its flavors.
3. Pour in the coconut milk and vegetable broth. Add the sweet potato, broccoli, mushrooms, and red bell pepper.

4. Bring to a boil, then reduce heat and simmer for 15 minutes or until the vegetables are tender.

Grilled Chicken With Steamed Asparagus

Ingredients:

- 2 tablespoons of olive oil
- 1 teaspoon of dried Italian seasoning
- Salt and pepper to taste
- 2 boneless, skinless chicken breasts
- 1 bunch asparagus, ends trimmed
- Lemon wedges for serving

Directions:

1. Preheat the grill to medium heat.
2. Rub the chicken breasts with olive oil, dried Italian seasoning, salt, and pepper.
3. Grill the chicken for 68 minutes per side or until cooked through.
4. While the chicken is grilling, steam the asparagus until tendercrisp.
5. Serve the grilled chicken with steamed asparagus.
6. Squeeze lemon juice over the chicken and asparagus before serving.

Turkey Meatballs With Zucchini Noodles

Ingredients:

- 1 clove garlic, minced
- 1 egg, beaten
- Salt and pepper to taste
- 2 zucchini, spiralized into noodles
- 1 cup marinara sauce
- 8 ounces lean ground turkey
- 1/4 cup almond flour
- 1/4 cup grated Parmesan cheese
- 1/4 cup chopped fresh parsley

- 1/4 cup diced onion

- 1 tablespoon olive oil

Directions:

1. In a bowl, combine ground turkey, almond flour, grated Parmesan cheese, chopped fresh parsley, diced onion, minced garlic, beaten egg, salt, and pepper.
2. Mix well.
3. Shape the turkey mixture into small meatballs.
4. Heat olive oil in a skillet over medium heat.
5. Add the meatballs to the skillet and cook for 1012 minutes, turning occasionally, until browned and cooked through. Remove the meatballs from the skillet and set aside.
6. In the same skillet, add the spiralized zucchini noodles and sauté for 34 minutes until tender.

7. Pour the marinara sauce over the zucchini noodles and heat until warmed.
8. Serve the turkey meatballs on top of the zucchini noodles.

Tofu And Vegetable Kebabs With A Side Of Couscous

Ingredients:

- Lemon juice

- Dried oregano

- Salt and pepper to taste

- Firm tofu, cubed

- Assorted vegetables (bell peppers, cherry tomatoes, zucchini, red onion, etc.)

- Olive oil

- Couscous, cooked according to package
DIRECTIONS:

Directions:

1. Preheat the grill to mediumhigh heat.
2. Assemble the tofu and vegetable cubes onto skewers.
3. Brush the kebabs with olive oil and season with salt, pepper, and dried oregano.
4. Grill the kebabs for 810 minutes, rotating occasionally, until the tofu is lightly browned and the vegetables are tender.
5. In a bowl, fluff the cooked couscous with a fork and drizzle with olive oil and lemon juice. Season with salt and pepper.
6. Serve the tofu and vegetable kebabs on a bed of couscous.

Spinach And Mushroom Frittata With A Green Salad:

Ingredients:

- 6 large eggs
- 1/2 cup of shredded cheese (cheddar, feta, etc.)
- Salt and pepper to taste
- Olive oil
- Mixed greens for the salad
- 1 cup of fresh spinach leaves
- 1 cup of sliced mushrooms
- 1/2 onion, finely chopped

- Balsamic vinaigrette or lemontahini dressing

Directions:

1. Preheat the oven to 375°F (190°C).
2. In an ovensafe skillet, sauté the chopped onion and sliced mushrooms in olive oil until softened.
3. Add the fresh spinach leaves and cook until wilted.
4. In a bowl, whisk the eggs, shredded cheese, salt, and pepper.
5. Pour the egg mixture into the skillet over the sautéed vegetables.
6. Cook on the stovetop for a few minutes until the edges are set.
7. Transfer the skillet to the preheated oven and bake for 1015 minutes or until the frittata is fully set and slightly browned.

8. Prepare a green salad with mixed greens and dress with balsamic vinaigrette or lemon tahini dressing.
9. Slice the frittata and serve with the green salad.

Almond And Coconut Energy Bites

Ingredients:

- 1 cup ground almonds
- 1/2 cup unsweetened shredded coconut
- 1 teaspoon vanilla extract
- A pinch of sea salt
- 6 pitted Medjool dates

Directions:

1. In a food processor, mix all Ingredients: until thoroughly incorporated.
2. Form into little balls.
3. Chill for 1 hour before serving.

Berry Greek Yogurt Parfait

Ingredients:

- 1 teaspoon raw honey
- 1 cup Greek yogurt (unsweetened)
- 1/2 cup fresh mixed berries
- 1 tablespoon chia seeds

Directions:

1. In a glass, layer Greek yogurt and berries.
2. Garnish with chia seeds.
3. Drizzle with raw honey to finish.

Apple Cinnamon Quinoa Porridge

Ingredients:

- 1 tablespoon honey
- 1/4 teaspoon ground cinnamon
- 1/4 teaspoon ground nutmeg
- 2 tablespoons chopped almonds
- 1/2 cup quinoa
- 1 cup almond milk
- 1/2 cup diced apple
- 2 tablespoons dried cranberries

Directions:

1. In a medium saucepan, combine the quinoa and almond milk.
2. Bring to a low simmer and cook for 10 minutes, stirring occasionally.
3. Add the diced apple, honey, cinnamon, and nutmeg. Simmer for an additional 3 minutes.
4. Remove from heat and stir in the almonds and cranberries. Serve warm.

Baked Egg Cups

Ingredients:

- 1/4 cup diced onion
- 1/4 cup diced mushrooms
- 1/4 cup shredded cheese
- 1/4 teaspoon sea salt
- 4 large eggs
- 1/4 cup diced bell pepper
- 1/4 teaspoon black pepper

Directions:

1. Preheat oven to 350°F. Grease 4 muffin cups.

2. In a medium bowl, whisk together the eggs, bell pepper, onion, mushrooms, cheese, salt, and pepper.
3. Divide the egg mixture evenly among the muffin cups.
4. Bake for 15 minutes, or until the eggs are set. Serve warm.

Breakfast Burritos

Ingredients:

- 1/4 cup diced onion
- 1/4 cup diced mushrooms
- 1/4 cup shredded cheese
- 4 whole wheat tortillas
- 1/4 teaspoon sea salt
- 4 large eggs
- 1/4 cup diced bell pepper
- 1/4 teaspoon black pepper

Directions:

1. In a medium bowl, whisk together the eggs, bell pepper, onion, mushrooms, cheese, salt, and pepper.
2. Heat a large skillet over medium heat.
3. Add the egg mixture and cook, stirring occasionally, until the eggs are cooked through.
4. Divide the egg mixture among the tortillas. Roll up the burritos and serve.

Salmon With Teriyaki Glaze And Brown Rice

Ingredients:

Applied to the Teriyaki Glaze:

- 1/4 cup tamari or soy sauce

- 2 teaspoons of mirin (a sweet rice wine from Japan).

- 1 tablespoon brown sugar or honey

- 1 teaspoon fresh ginger and garlic, both finely chopped

- 1 teaspoon cornstarch, optionally used to thicken the mixture.

- 2 salmon filets, each weighing around 6 ounces

Regarding the brown rice:

- 1 serving of brown rice

- 2 cups water 1/8 teaspoon of salt

Directions:

1. Combine the soy sauce or tamari, mirin, honey or brown sugar, chopped ginger, and minced garlic in a small bowl. Add cornstarch to the recipe if you want a thicker glaze.
2. Spread half of the teriyaki glaze over the salmon filets on a shallow plate. Put the other half away for some other time.
3. For around 15 to 20 minutes, marinate the salmon in the glaze.
4. Run a cold water rinse over the brown rice while the salmon is marinating. The washed rice, water, and a dash of salt should all be put

together in a medium pot. Bring to a boil, lower the heat to a simmer, cover the pot, and cook for 40 to 45 minutes, or until the rice is cooked through and the water has been absorbed.
5. Turn the heat to mediumhigh and preheat the grill or grill pan.
6. Grill the salmon filets with the marinade for 4 to 5 minutes on each side, or until the fish is cooked through and flakes easily. While frying the fish, baste it with the teriyaki glaze that was saved.
7. Steam the veggies of your choosing while the salmon is roasting.
8. Take the salmon off the grill when it's finished cooking.
9. Spoon cooked brown rice over the salmon with teriyaki glaze.

10. Drizzle the fish and rice with the leftover teriyaki glaze.
11. Add sesame seeds and thinly sliced green onions as a garnish.

Portobello Mushrooms Stuffed With Feta And Spinach

Ingredients:

- 4 big Portobello mushrooms, cleaned and with stems removed 2 cups chopped fresh spinach 1/2 cup crumbled feta cheese 1/4 cup diced red onion 2 cloves minced garlic

- Olive oil, 1 tbsp

- Salt and pepper to taste Optional topping of grated Parmesan cheese

- Fresh parsley chopped finely for garnish

Directions:

1. Set the oven temperature to 375°F (190°C).

2. Arrange the cleaned Portobello mushrooms, gill side up, on a baking sheet.
3. Heat the olive oil in a pan over medium heat. Add the minced garlic and red onion, both diced. The onion should be transparent after 2 to 3 minutes of sautéing.
4. Fill the skillet with the chopped spinach. To wilt the spinach, continue to sauté for an additional 2 to 3 minutes.
5. Turn off the heat and let the spinach mixture gradually cool.
6. Add the feta cheese crumbles. To taste, add salt and pepper to the blend.
7. Gently push the spinach and feta mixture into each Portobello mushroom's gill side after spooning it in evenly.
8. If preferred, top each filled mushroom with a little grated Parmesan cheese.

9. Put the baking sheet with the stuffing for the mushrooms in the oven.
10. Bake for 15-20 minutes, or until the cheese is melted and bubbling, and the mushrooms are soft.
11. Take the filled mushrooms out of the oven, then allow them to cool before serving.
12. Before serving, garnish with freshly cut parsley.

Grilled Chicken Wrap

Ingredients:

- Mixed greens

- Sliced tomato

- Sliced red onion

- 4 oz grilled chicken breast, sliced
- Whole grain tortilla
- Greek yogurtbased dressing

Directions:

1. Lay the tortilla flat and layer grilled chicken, mixed greens, sliced tomato, and red onion.
2. Drizzle with Greek yogurtbased dressing.
3. Roll up the tortilla tightly and cut in half.

Lentil Soup

Ingredients:

- ½ cup diced onion
- 2 cups lowsodium vegetable broth
- 1 tsp olive oil
- ½ tsp dried thyme
- 1 cup cooked lentils
- ½ cup diced carrots
- ½ cup diced celery
- Salt and pepper to taste

Directions:

1. In a pot, heat olive oil over medium heat.
2. Add diced carrots, celery, and onion. Sauté until vegetables are softened.
3. Add cooked lentils, vegetable broth, dried thyme, salt, and pepper.
4. Cook for 15 to 20 minutes after bringing to a simmer.
5. Serve hot.

Buckwheat Pancakes With A Dollop Of Greek Yogurt And Sliced Almonds:

Ingredients:

- 1 tablespoon honey or maple syrup
- 1 cup milk (dairy or plantbased)
- 1 large egg
- 1 tablespoon melted butter or oil
- 1 cup buckwheat flour
- 1 tablespoon baking powder
- Greek yogurt and sliced almonds for topping

Directions:

1. In a large bowl, whisk together the buckwheat flour and baking powder.
2. In a separate bowl, whisk together the honey or maple syrup, milk, egg, and melted butter or oil.
3. Pour the wet Ingredients:into the dry Ingredients:and stir until just combined. Be careful not to overmix; a few lumps are okay.
4. Heat a nonstick skillet or griddle over medium heat and lightly grease it with butter or oil.
5. Ladle about 1/4 cup of batter onto the skillet for each pancake.
6. Cook until bubbles form on the surface of the pancake, then flip and cook for another 12 minutes until golden brown.
7. Repeat with the remaining batter.
8. Serve the pancakes with a dollop of Greek yogurt and sliced almonds on top.

Veggie And Cheese Wrap Using A Whole Grain Tortilla:

Ingredients:

- 1 whole grain tortilla
- Assorted chopped vegetables (e.g., bell peppers, tomatoes, cucumbers)
- Grated cheese of your choice
- Hummus or any preferred spread

Directions:

1. Lay the whole grain tortilla flat on a clean surface.

2. Spread a layer of hummus or your preferred spread evenly on the tortilla.
3. Sprinkle the chopped vegetables and grated cheese on top of the spread.
4. Roll the tortilla tightly, enclosing the filling.
5. Cut the wrap in half, if desired.
6. Serve and enjoy.

Mediterranean Orange And Almond Cake

Ingredients:

- 1/2 cup of honey
- 1 teaspoon of baking powder
- 1/4 teaspoon of salt
- 2 oranges
- 4 eggs
- 1 cup of almond flour
- Powdered sugar for dusting (optional)

Directions:

1. Preheat the oven to 350°F (175°C). Grease a round cake pan and set aside.
2. Wash the oranges, then place them in a pot of water and bring to a boil. Simmer for about 1 hour until the oranges are soft.
3. Drain the oranges and let them cool. Cut them into quarters and remove any seeds.
4. In a blender or food processor, combine the boiled oranges (including the peel) and eggs. Blend until smooth.
5. In a mixing bowl, whisk together the almond flour, honey, baking powder, and salt. Add the orange mixture and mix until well combined.
6. Pour the batter into the prepared cake pan and smooth the top.
7. Bake for about 4045 minutes, or until a toothpick inserted into the center comes out clean.

8. Remove from the oven and let the cake cool in the pan for 10 minutes. Then transfer to a wire rack to cool completely.
9. Dust with powdered sugar, if desired, before serving.

Ayurvedic Greek Yogurt With Honey And Walnuts

Ingredients:

- 1 cup of Greek yogurt
- 2 tablespoons of honey
- 1/4 cup of chopped walnuts

Directions:

1. In a bowl, scoop the Greek yogurt.
2. Drizzle honey over the yogurt.
3. Sprinkle the chopped walnuts on top.
4. Mix gently to combine all the ingredients.
5. Serve immediately.

Ayurvedic Fig And Date Energy Balls

Ingredients:

- 1 cup of almonds
- 1 tablespoon of coconut oil
- 1 tablespoon of honey
- 1/2 teaspoon of ground cinnamon
- 1 cup of dried figs
- 1 cup of dates
- Shredded coconut for coating (optional)

Directions:

1. In a food processor, combine the dried figs, dates, almonds, coconut oil, honey, and ground cinnamon.
2. Process the mixture until it forms a sticky dough.
3. Scoop out tablespoonsized portions of the dough and roll them into balls.
4. If desired, roll the balls in shredded coconut to coat the exterior.
5. Place the energy balls on a tray lined with parchment paper and refrigerate for at least 30 minutes to firm up.
6. Store the energy balls in an airtight container in the refrigerator.

Cauliflower Crust Pizza

Ingredients:

- 1/2 teaspoon dried basil
- 1/2 teaspoon garlic powder
- 1/4 teaspoon salt
- 1/4 teaspoon black pepper
- 1 egg, beaten
- Pizza sauce
- 1 medium cauliflower head, florets only
- 1/2 cup grated Parmesan cheese
- 1/2 teaspoon dried oregano

- Mozzarella cheese

- Toppings of your choice (e.g., sliced tomatoes, spinach, mushrooms, olives)

Directions:

1. Preheat the oven to 450°F (230°C) and line a baking sheet with parchment paper.
2. In a food processor, pulse the cauliflower florets until they resemble fine crumbs.
3. Transfer the cauliflower crumbs to a microwavesafe bowl and microwave on high for 56 minutes until tender.
4. Allow the cauliflower to cool slightly, then transfer it to a clean kitchen towel. Squeeze out as much liquid as possible from the cauliflower.
5. In a bowl, combine the cauliflower crumbs, grated Parmesan cheese, dried oregano, dried

basil, garlic powder, salt, black pepper, and beaten egg. Mix well until a dough forms.
6. Place the cauliflower dough on the prepared baking sheet and press it into a round shape, about 1/4inch thick.
7. Bake the cauliflower crust in the preheated oven for about 15 minutes or until it is golden brown and crispy.
8. Remove the crust from the oven and spread pizza sauce over the surface.
9. Sprinkle with mozzarella cheese and add your desired toppings.
10. Return the pizza to the oven and bake for an additional 57 minutes or until the cheese is melted and bubbly.
11. Slice and serve the cauliflower crust pizza as a healthier alternative to traditional pizza.

Spinach And Mushroom Omelet:

Ingredients:

- 1 teaspoon olive oil
- 1 cup fresh spinach leaves
- 1/4 cup sliced mushrooms
- 2 large eggs
- 1 tablespoon milk
- Salt and pepper to taste
- 2 tablespoons grated Parmesan cheese

Directions:

1. In a bowl, whisk together eggs, milk, salt, and pepper.

2. Heat olive oil in a nonstick skillet over medium heat.
3. Add fresh spinach leaves and sliced mushrooms to the skillet. Cook for about 23 minutes or until the spinach wilts and the mushrooms are tender.
4. Pour the beaten egg mixture into the skillet, swirling it around to cover the vegetables evenly.
5. Cook the omelet for 23 minutes or until the edges are set and the bottom is lightly browned.
6. Sprinkle grated Parmesan cheese over half of the omelet.
7. Use a spatula to fold the omelet in half, covering the cheese.

8. Cook for an additional 12 minutes until the cheese is melted and the omelet is cooked through.
9. Transfer the omelet to a plate and serve hot.

Salad Of Black Beans And Quinoa With Avocado Dressing

Ingredients:

- Cherry tomatoes, halved
- Diced cucumber
- Diced red onion
- Chopped fresh cilantro
- 1 avocado
- Juice of 1 lime

- 1/2 cup cooked quinoa
- 1/2 cup black beans (canned or cooked)
- Mixed salad greens
- Salt and pepper to taste

Directions:

1. In a bowl, combine the cooked quinoa, black beans, mixed salad greens, cherry tomatoes, cucumber, red onion, and cilantro.
2. In a separate bowl, mash the avocado with lime juice, salt, and pepper to make the dressing.
3. Pour the avocado dressing over the quinoa and black bean salad and toss to coat.

Grilled Chicken Breast With Greek Salad

Ingredients:

- Diced red onion
- Kalamata olives
- Feta cheese, crumbled
- Olive oil
- Lemon juice
- Dried oregano
- 1 chicken breast
- Mixed salad greens
- Cherry tomatoes, halved

- Diced cucumber

- Salt and pepper to taste

Directions:

1. Season the chicken breast with olive oil, lemon juice, dried oregano, salt, and pepper.
2. The chicken should be cooked through after grilling it for 6 to 8 minutes on each side.
3. In a bowl, combine the mixed salad greens, cherry tomatoes, cucumber, red onion, Kalamata olives, and crumbled feta cheese.
4. Drizzle with olive oil and lemon juice. Season with salt, pepper, and dried oregano.
5. Slice the grilled chicken breast and serve it on top of the Greek salad.

Lentil And Vegetable Stirfry

Ingredients:

- Minced garlic
- Grated ginger
- Lowsodium soy sauce or tamari
- Sesame oil
- 1/2 cup cooked lentils
- Assorted stirfry vegetables (such as bell peppers, broccoli, and snap peas)
- Salt and pepper to taste

Directions:

1. In a pan, heat sesame oil over mediumhigh heat.

2. Add minced garlic and grated ginger, and stirfry for 1 minute.
3. Add the stirfry vegetables and cook until crisptender.
4. Stir in the cooked lentils and season with lowsodium soy sauce or tamari, salt, and pepper.

Broccoli And Cauliflower Soup.

Ingredients:

- 1 onion, chopped
- 2 cloves garlic, minced
- 4 cups vegetable broth
- 1 cup water
- Salt and pepper to taste
- 1 head broccoli, chopped
- 1 head cauliflower, chopped
- Olive oil for sautéing

Directions:

1. Using a large pot, heat the olive oil on medium heat.
2. Add chopped onion and minced garlic, and sauté until softened and fragrant.
3. Add chopped broccoli and cauliflower to the pot, and stir for a few minutes.
4. Pour vegetable broth and water into the pot, and bring to a boil.
5. Reduce the heat to a simmer, cover the pot, and let the soup cook until the vegetables are tender.
6. Use an immersion blender or transfer the soup to a blender to puree the mixture until smooth.
7. Season the Broccoli and Cauliflower Soup with salt and pepper according to your taste preference.

8. Let the soup simmer for a few minutes more so the flavors can meld.
9. Serve the comforting and nourishing Broccoli and Cauliflower Soup hot, garnished with fresh herbs or a drizzle of olive oil if desired.

Spinach And Mushroom Quiche.

Ingredients:

- 1/2 cup shredded cheese such as Swiss or cheddar
- 4 large eggs
- 1 cup milk (dairy or plantbased)
- 1 prepared pie crust, either homemade or purchased
- 1 cup fresh spinach, chopped
- 1 cup mushrooms, sliced
- Salt and pepper to taste

Directions:

1. Preheat the oven to 375°F (190°C).
2. Place the premade pie crust in a pie dish and set it aside.
3. In a pan, sauté chopped spinach and sliced mushrooms until they are cooked and any excess liquid has evaporated.
4. Spread the cooked spinach and mushrooms evenly over the pie crust.
5. Sprinkle shredded cheese on top of the spinach and mushrooms.
6. In a bowl, whisk together eggs, milk, salt, and pepper until well combined.
7. Pour the egg mixture over the vegetables and cheese in the pie crust.
8. Carefully transfer the quiche to the preheated oven and bake for about 30 35 minutes or until the quiche i s set and lightly golden on top.

9. Before slicing and serving, take the quiche out of the oven and allow it cool somewhat.

Mexican Quinoa Skillet

Ingredients:

- 1 tsp chili powder

- 1 cup quinoa, rinsed

- 1 can (14 ounces) black beans, rinsed and drained

- 1 can (14 ounces) diced tomatoes with green chilies

- 1 cup vegetable broth

- Salt and pepper to taste

- Fresh cilantro, chopped (for garnish)

- 1 tbsp olive oil

- 1 onion, diced
- 1 red bell pepper, diced
- 1 jalapeno pepper, seeded and minced
- 3 cloves garlic, minced
- 1 tsp ground cumin
- Avocado slices (for garnish)

Directions:

1. Heat olive oil in a large skillet over medium heat. Add the onion, red bell pepper, and jalapeno pepper.
2. Sauté until the vegetables are tender.
3. Stir in the garlic, cumin, and chili powder. Cook for 1 minute until fragrant.

4. Add the quinoa, black beans, diced tomatoes with green chilies, and vegetable broth to the skillet.
5. Bring to a boil, then reduce heat and simmer for 15 minutes or until the quinoa is cooked and the liquid is absorbed.
6. Season with salt and pepper to taste. Garnish with fresh cilantro and avocado slices before serving.

Mediterranean Lentil Soup

Ingredients:

- 1 cup dried green or brown lentils, rinsed
- 4 cups vegetable broth
- 1 tsp dried oregano
- 1 tsp dried thyme
- Salt and pepper to taste
- Fresh parsley, chopped (for garnish)
- 1 tbsp olive oil
- 1 onion, chopped
- 3 cloves garlic, minced

- 2 carrots, diced
- 2 stalks celery, diced
- 1 can (14 ounces) diced tomatoes
- Lemon wedges (for serving)

Directions:

1. Heat olive oil in a large pot over medium heat. Add the onion, garlic, carrots, and celery. Sauté until the vegetables are softened.
2. Stir in the diced tomatoes, lentils, vegetable broth, dried oregano, and dried thyme. Bring to a boil, then reduce heat and simmer for 30 minutes or until the lentils are tender.
3. Season with salt and pepper to taste. Serve the Mediterranean Lentil Soup hot, garnished with fresh parsley and lemon wedges.

Caprese Stuffed Portobello Mushrooms

Ingredients:

- 1/4 cup sliced fresh mozzarella cheese
- 2 tablespoons chopped fresh basil
- 1 tablespoon balsamic vinegar
- 1 tablespoon olive oil
- 2 large Portobello mushrooms
- 1/2 cup cherry tomatoes, halved
- Salt and pepper to taste

Directions:

1. Preheat the oven to 400°F (200°C).

2. Remove the stems from the Portobello mushrooms and gently scrape out the gills.
3. In a small bowl, combine halved cherry tomatoes, sliced fresh mozzarella cheese, chopped fresh basil, balsamic vinegar, olive oil, salt, and pepper.
4. Spoon the tomato and mozzarella mixture into the cavity of each mushroom.
5. Place the stuffed mushrooms on a baking sheet lined with parchment paper.
6. Bake for 2025 minutes or until the mushrooms are tender and the cheese is melted and slightly golden.
7. Remove from the oven and let them cool for a few minutes before serving.

Chicken Lettuce Wraps

Ingredients:

- 1 tablespoon hoisin sauce
- 1 tablespoon rice vinegar
- 1 tablespoon sesame oil
- 1 clove garlic, minced
- 1/2 teaspoon grated ginger
- 8 ounces ground chicken
- 1/4 cup diced red bell pepper
- 1/4 cup diced water chestnuts
- 2 tablespoons lowsodium soy sauce

- 4 large lettuce leaves (e.g., Bibb or iceberg)

Directions:

1. In a skillet, heat sesame oil over medium heat.
2. Add minced garlic and grated ginger to the skillet. Sauté for 12 minutes until fragrant.
3. Add ground chicken to the skillet and cook until browned and cooked through.
4. Stir in diced red bell pepper and water chestnuts. Cook for an additional 23
5. minutes.
6. In a small bowl, whisk together lowsodium soy sauce, hoisin sauce, and rice vinegar.
7. Pour the sauce mixture into the skillet with the chicken and vegetables. Stir to coat evenly.
8. Cook for another 12 minutes until heated through.

9. Spoon the chicken mixture onto lettuce leaves, dividing it evenly.
10. Wrap the lettuce leaves around the filling to form lettuce wraps. Serve

Cauliflower Fried Rice

Ingredients:

- 1/4 cup diced onion
- 2 cloves garlic, minced
- 2 tablespoons lowsodium soy sauce
- 1 tablespoon sesame oil
- 1 tablespoon olive oil
- 2 cups cauliflower rice
- 8 ounces cooked shrimp, peeled and deveined
- 1/2 cup diced carrots
- 1/2 cup frozen peas

- 2 eggs, beaten

Directions:

1. In a large skillet, heat olive oil over medium heat.
2. Add minced garlic and diced onion to the skillet. Sauté for 12 minutes until fragrant.
3. Add diced carrots and frozen peas to the skillet. Cook for 34 minutes until the vegetables are tender.
4. Push the vegetables to one side of the skillet and pour the beaten eggs into the other side.
5. Scramble the eggs until cooked through, then mix them together with the vegetables.
6. Add cauliflower rice and cooked shrimp to the skillet. Stir to combine.

7. Drizzle lowsodium soy sauce and sesame oil over the mixture. Stir to coat evenly. Cook for another 34 minutes
8. Season with salt and pepper to taste. Serve hot.

Black Bean And Sweet Potato Tacos With A Side Of Guacamole

Ingredients:

- 1 teaspoon of chili powder
- 1/2 teaspoon of ground cumin
- Salt and pepper to taste
- Wholegrain taco shells or tortillas
- 1 can of black beans, drained and rinsed
- 2 mediumsized sweet potatoes, peeled and diced
- 1 tablespoon of olive oil
- Guacamole (storebought or homemade)

Directions:

1. Preheat the oven to 400°F (200°C).
2. Toss the diced sweet potatoes with olive oil, chili powder, ground cumin, salt, and pepper.
3. Spread the seasoned sweet potatoes on a baking sheet and roast in the oven for 20-25 minutes or until tender and slightly crispy.
4. While the sweet potatoes are roasting, heat the black beans in a small saucepan over medium heat until warmed through.
5. Warm the taco shells or tortillas in the oven according to package instructions.
6. Assemble the tacos by layering the black beans, roasted sweet potatoes, and guacamole inside the taco shells.
7. Serve with a side of extra guacamole if desired.

Sautéed Shrimp With Zucchini Noodles And Pesto Sauce

Ingredients:

- 2 tablespoons of pesto sauce (storebought or homemade)

- Olive oil

- Salt and pepper to taste

- Fresh or frozen shrimp, peeled and deveined

- Zucchini, spiralized into noodles

- Grated Parmesan cheese (optional)

Directions:

1. In a large skillet, heat some olive oil over medium heat.
2. Sauté the shrimp until they turn pink and are fully cooked.
3. Add the spiralized zucchini noodles to the skillet and cook for a few minutes until they are tendercrisp.
4. Stir in the pesto sauce, coating the shrimp and zucchini noodles evenly.
5. Season with salt and pepper to taste.
6. Serve the sautéed shrimp and zucchini noodles with a sprinkle of grated Parmesan cheese if desired.

Cauliflower Rice Stirfry With Tofu And Mixed Vegetables

Ingredients:

- Lowsodium soy sauce or tamari
- Sesame oil
- Grated ginger
- Minced garlic
- 1 block of firm tofu, cubed
- Cauliflower rice (storebought or homemade by pulsing cauliflower florets in a food processor)
- Mixed stirfry vegetables (broccoli, bell peppers, snap peas, carrots, etc.)

- Sesame seeds (optional)

Directions:

1. In a large skillet or wok, heat some sesame oil over mediumhigh heat.
2. Add the cubed tofu and cook until lightly browned on all sides.
3. Stir in the mixed stirfry vegetables and cook until they are tendercrisp.
4. Add the cauliflower rice to the skillet and stirfry for a few minutes until heated through.
5. Season with lowsodium soy sauce or tamari, grated ginger, and minced garlic.
6. Sprinkle with sesame seeds if desired and serve.

Cinnamonroasted Chickpeas

Ingredients:

- 1 cup cooked chickpeas (drained and rinsed)
- 1 teaspoon olive oil
- 1 teaspoon cinnamon
- 2 tsp raw honey

Directions:

1. Combine chickpeas, olive oil, cinnamon, and honey in a mixing bowl.
2. Arrange on a baking sheet.
3. Roast for 4045 minutes, or until crisp, at 375°F (190°C).

Dark Chocolate Avocado Mousse

Ingredients:

- 2 tablespoons maple syrup
- 1 teaspoon vanilla extract
- 1 ripe avocado
- 2 tbsp raw cocoa powder
- 70% cocoa dark chocolate (50g melted)

Directions:

1. In a food processor, combine all Ingredients: and pulse until smooth.
2. Place in the refrigerator for at least 2 hours before serving.

Spiced Pumpkin Seeds

Ingredients:

- 1/2 cup pumpkin seeds

- 1 teaspoon olive oil

- Paprika (1/2 teaspoon)

- 1/4 teaspoon sea salt

Directions:

1. Combine seeds, olive oil, paprika, and salt in a mixing bowl.
2. Bake for 1215 minutes, or until brown, at 350°F (175°C).

Mediterranean Quinoa Bowl

Ingredients:

- 1/4 cup diced cucumber
- 2 tablespoons chopped fresh parsley
- 2 tablespoons freshly squeezed lemon juice
- 1 tablespoon extravirgin olive oil
- 1 cup cooked quinoa
- 1/4 cup crumbled feta cheese
- 2 tablespoons diced red onion
- Salt and pepper to taste

Directions:

1. In a medium bowl, combine the cooked quinoa, feta cheese, red onion, cucumber, and parsley.
2. In a small bowl, whisk together the lemon juice, olive oil, salt, and pepper.
3. Pour the dressing over the quinoa mixture and toss to combine.
4. Serve immediately or store in the refrigerator for up to 3 days.

Eggplant Lasagna

Ingredients:

- 1 teaspoon dried basil
- 1/2 teaspoon red pepper flakes
- 1/2 cup ricotta cheese
- 1/2 cup shredded mozzarella cheese
- 1/4 cup grated Parmesan cheese
- 1/4 cup chopped fresh parsley
- 2 tablespoons extravirgin olive oil
- 1 large eggplant, sliced into 1/4inch rounds
- 1/2 cup chopped onion

- 4 cloves garlic, minced

- 1 can (28 ounces) crushed tomatoes

- 1 teaspoon dried oregano

Directions:

1. Preheat oven to 375F.
2. Heat olive oil in a large skillet over medium heat. Add eggplant and onion and cook, stirring occasionally, until eggplant is lightly browned, about 8 minutes. Add garlic and cook for 1 minute.
3. Add tomatoes, oregano, basil, and red pepper flakes and simmer for 10 minutes.
4. Spread a thin layer of tomato sauce in the bottom of a 9x13inch baking dish. Layer half of the eggplant slices over the sauce.

5. Spread half of the ricotta cheese over the eggplant and top with half of the mozzarella and Parmesan cheeses. Repeat the layers with the remaining Ingredients: and top with the remaining Parmesan cheese.
6. Bake for 20 minutes, or until the cheese is melted and bubbly. Sprinkle with parsley and serve.

Chickpea Curry

Ingredients:

- 1 teaspoon ground coriander
- 1 teaspoon ground turmeric
- 1 teaspoon ground ginger
- 1/4 teaspoon cayenne pepper
- 1 can (15 ounces) chickpeas, drained and rinsed
- 1 can (14.5 ounces) diced tomatoes
- 1/2 cup vegetable broth
- 1/4 cup chopped fresh cilantro
- 1 tablespoon extravirgin olive oil

- 1 onion, diced
- 2 cloves garlic, minced
- 1 teaspoon ground cumin
- Salt and pepper to taste

Directions:

1. Heat the olive oil in a large skillet over medium heat. Add the onion and garlic and cook, stirring occasionally, until the onion is softened, about 5 minutes.
2. Add the cumin, coriander, turmeric, ginger, and cayenne pepper and cook for 1 minute longer.
3. Add the chickpeas, tomatoes, broth, and cilantro and bring to a simmer.

4. Reduce the heat to low and simmer for 10 minutes, stirring occasionally, until the sauce has thickened.
5. Season with salt and pepper to taste and serve.

Quinoa And Chickpea Salad

Ingredients:

- ¼ cup diced red bell pepper
- 2 tbsp crumbled feta cheese
- ½ cup cooked quinoa
- ½ cup canned chickpeas, rinsed and drained ¼ cup diced cucumber
- 2 tbsp lemon vinaigrette dressing

Directions:

1. In a bowl, combine cooked quinoa, chickpeas, cucumber, red bell pepper, and feta cheese.
2. Drizzle with lemon vinaigrette dressing and toss well.

3. Chill in the refrigerator before serving.

Tuna And Avocado Salad

Ingredients:

- ½ cup cherry tomatoes, halved
- 2 tbsp balsamic vinaigrette dressing
- 1 can tuna in water, drained
- ½ avocado, diced
- 1 cup mixed salad greens

Directions:

1. In a bowl, combine drained tuna, diced avocado, mixed salad greens, and cherry tomatoes.
2. Drizzle with balsamic vinaigrette dressing.
3. Toss well and enjoy.

Ayurvedic Pistachio Rosewater Cookies

Ingredients:

- 2 tablespoons of honey
- 1 tablespoon of rosewater
- 1/2 teaspoon of baking powder
- A pinch of salt
- 1 cup of almond flour
- 1/4 cup of coconut flour
- 1/4 cup of pistachios, finely chopped
- 1/4 cup of coconut oil, melted

Directions:

1. Preheat the oven to 350°F (175°C). Line a baking sheet with parchment paper.
2. In a mixing bowl, combine the almond flour, coconut flour, chopped pistachios, baking powder, and salt.
3. In a separate bowl, whisk together the melted coconut oil, honey, and rosewater.
4. Add the wet Ingredients:to the dry Ingredients:and mix until well combined.
5. Roll the dough into tablespoonsized balls and place them on the prepared baking sheet. Flatten each ball slightly with the palm of your hand.
6. Bake for about 1215 minutes, or until the edges are golden brown.
7. Remove from the oven and let the cookies cool on the baking sheet for a few minutes

before transferring them to a wire rack to cool completely.

Mediterranean Yogurt Parfait With Fresh Berries

Ingredients:

- 2 tablespoons of honey
- 2 tablespoons of chopped nuts (such as almonds or walnuts)
- 1 cup of Greek yogurt
- 1 cup of mixed fresh berries (such as strawberries, blueberries, and raspberries)

Directions:

1. In a glass or jar, layer half of the Greek yogurt.
2. Add half of the mixed fresh berries on top of the yogurt.
3. Drizzle 1 tablespoon of honey over the berries.

4. Repeat the layers with the remaining yogurt, berries, and honey.
5. Sprinkle the chopped nuts on the top layer.
6. Serve immediately.

Ayurvedic Date And Walnut Pudding

Ingredients:

- 1 cup of coconut milk
- 2 tablespoons of honey
- 1/2 teaspoon of ground cardamom
- 1/4 teaspoon of ground cinnamon
- 1 cup of pitted dates
- 1 cup of walnuts
- Shredded coconut for garnish (optional)

Directions:

1. In a food processor, combine the pitted dates, walnuts, coconut milk, honey, ground cardamom, and ground cinnamon.
2. Process the mixture until smooth and creamy.
3. Divide the pudding mixture into serving bowls or glasses.
4. Cover and refrigerate for at least 2 hours to allow the pudding to set.
5. Before serving, garnish with shredded coconut, if desired.

Shrimp And Vegetable Kebabs:

Ingredients:

- 1 tablespoon lemon juice
- 1 clove garlic, minced
- 1/2 teaspoon dried oregano
- Salt and pepper to taste
- 1/2 cup cherry tomatoes
- 1/2 cup bell peppers, cut into chunks
- 8 oz shrimp, peeled and deveined
- 1 tablespoon olive oil
- 1/2 cup zucchini, sliced into rounds

Directions:

1. In a bowl, whisk together olive oil, lemon juice, minced garlic, dried oregano, salt, and pepper.
2. Add shrimp to the bowl and toss to coat them in the marinade. Let them marinate for about 1520 minutes.
3. Preheat the grill or grill pan over mediumhigh heat.
4. Thread themarinated shrimp, cherry tomatoes, bell peppers, and zucchini onto skewers, alternating the ingredients.
5. Grill the shrimp and vegetable skewers for about 23 minutes per side or until the shrimp are cooked through and the vegetables are tender.
6. Remove the skewers from the grill and serve hot.

Black Bean And Sweet Potato Chili:

Ingredients:

- 1 can (15 oz) black beans, rinsed and drained
- 1 can (14 oz) diced tomatoes
- 1 cup vegetable broth
- 1 teaspoon chili powder
- 1/2 teaspoon ground cumin
- Salt and pepper to taste
- Fresh cilantro for garnish (optional)
- 1 tablespoon olive oil
- 1/2 onion, diced

- 2 cloves garlic, minced

- 1 small sweet potato, peeled and diced

- Whole grain crackers for serving

Directions:

1. Heat olive oil in a large pot over medium heat.
2. Add diced onion and minced garlic, sauté until fragrant and translucent.
3. Add diced sweet potato to the pot and cook for about 5 minutes, stirring occasionally.
4. Stir in black beans, diced tomatoes (with their juice), vegetable broth, chili powder, and ground cumin.
5. Season with salt and pepper to taste.
6. Bring the chili to a boil, then reduce heat to low, cover, and simmer for about 2025 minutes or until the sweet potato is tender.

7. Remove from heat.
8. Garnish with fresh cilantro if desired.
9. Serve the black bean and sweet potato chili with whole grain crackers for a satisfying lunch.

Caprese Salad With Grilled Chicken Or Sliced Turkey Breast:

Ingredients:

- 4 oz fresh mozzarella cheese, sliced
- 1/4 cup fresh basil leaves
- 1 tablespoon balsamic glaze
- 1 tablespoon olive oil
- 4 oz grilled chicken breast or sliced turkey breast
- 1 cup cherry tomatoes, halved
- Salt and pepper to taste

Directions:

1. Arrange the grilled chicken breast or sliced turkey breast on a plate.
2. Top with cherry tomatoes and fresh mozzarella cheese.
3. Garnish with fresh basil leaves.
4. Drizzle balsamic glaze and olive oil over the salad.
5. Season with salt and pepper to taste.
6. Serve the caprese salad with grilled chicken or sliced turkey breast as a light and refreshing lunch option.

Turkey And Vegetable Lettuce Wraps

Ingredients:

- Diced zucchini
- Minced garlic
- Low sodium soy sauce or tamari
- Sesame oil
- 1/2 pound ground turkey
- Diced bell peppers
- Shredded carrots
- Lettuce leaves for wrapping

Directions:

1. In a pan, heat sesame oil over medium heat.

2. Add minced garlic and ground turkey, and cook until browned.
3. Add the diced bell peppers, shredded carrots, and diced zucchini, and cook until tender.
4. Stir in low sodium soy sauce or tamari, and cook for another minute.
5. Spoon the turkey and vegetable mixture onto lettuce leaves, and roll them up to create lettuce wraps.

Baked Sweet Potato With Black Bean Salsa

Ingredients:

- Diced tomatoes
- Diced red onion
- Chopped fresh cilantro
- Lime juice
- 1 medium sized sweet potato
- 1/2 cup black beans (canned or cooked)
- Salt and pepper to taste

Directions:

1. Preheat the oven to 400°F (200°C).

2. Pierce the sweet potato with a fork, and bake for 40 minutes or until tender.
3. In a bowl, combine the black beans, diced tomatoes, diced red onion, chopped cilantro, lime juice, salt, and pepper to make the salsa.
4. Slice the baked sweet potato lengthwise, and spoon the black bean salsa on top.

Veggie And Brown Rice Stir Fry

Ingredients:

- Grated ginger
- Low sodium soy sauce or tamari
- Sesame oil
- Cooked brown rice
- Assorted stir fry vegetables (such as broccoli, carrots, and snap peas)
- Minced garlic
- Salt and pepper to taste

Directions:

1. In a pan, heat sesame oil over mediumhigh heat.
2. Add minced garlic and grated ginger, and stirfry for 1 minute.
3. Add the stirfry vegetables and cook until crisptender.
4. Stir in the cooked brown rice and season with lowsodium soy sauce or tamari, salt, and pepper.

Roasted Beet And Goat Cheese Salad.

Ingredients:

- 1/4 cup crumbled goat cheese
- 2 tablespoons balsamic vinegar
- 2 tablespoons olive oil
- 2 large beets, peeled and cubed
- 2 cups mixed salad greens
- Salt and pepper to taste

Directions:

1. Preheat the oven to 400°F (200°C).
2. Olive oil, salt, and pepper should be added to the diced beets.

3. Roast the beets in the oven for about 30 minutes or until tender.
4. In a bowl, mix the roasted beets with mixed salad greens.
5. Drizzle balsamic vinegar and olive oil over the salad.
6. Top the salad with crumbled goat cheese.
7. Add pepper and salt to taste when seasoning.
8. Toss everything together until well combined.
9. Serve the Roasted Beet and Goat Cheese Salad as a refreshing and vibrant side dish or a light and delicious main meal.

Mango And Avocado Salad.

Ingredients:

- 1/4 cup chopped red onion
- 2 tablespoons lime juice
- 1 tablespoon chopped fresh cilantro
- 2 ripe mangoes, diced
- 1 ripe avocado, diced
- Salt and pepper to taste

Directions:

1. In a bowl, mix diced mangoes, diced avocado, chopped red onion, lime juice, and chopped cilantro.
2. Add pepper and salt to taste when seasoning.

3. Toss everything together until well combined.
4. Serve the Mango and Avocado Salad as a refreshing and delightful side dish or a flavorful and nutritious light meal.

Sesame Ginger Tofu Stir Fry.

Ingredients:

- 2 tablespoons soy sauce
- 1 tablespoon sesame oil
- 1 tablespoon grated ginger
- 1 block firm tofu, cubed
- 2 cups mixed stir fry vegetables (such as bell peppers, broccoli, and snow peas)
- 2 tablespoons sesame seeds

Directions:

1. In a pan, sauté cubed tofu and mixed stir fry vegetables with sesame oil until slightly tender.

2. Add grated ginger and continue to stir fry for a minute until fragrant.
3. Pour soy sauce over the tofu and vegetables, stirring to coat them evenly.
4. Sprinkle sesame seeds over the stir fry and continue to cook until vegetables are crisptender and tofu is heated through.
5. Serve the Sesame Ginger Tofu Stir Fry over cooked rice or noodles for a flavorful and satisfying meal.

Lemon Garlic Shrimp Stir Fry

Ingredients:

- 1 medium zucchini, sliced
- Juice of 1 lemon
- 1 tsp lemon zest
- Salt and pepper to taste
- 1 lb (450g) shrimp, peeled and deveined
- 2 tbsps olive oil
- 3 cloves garlic, minced
- 1 red bell pepper, sliced
- 1 yellow bell pepper, sliced

- Fresh parsley for garnish

Directions:

1. Heat the olive oil in a large skillet over medium heat. Add the minced garlic and sauté for 1 minute until fragrant.
2. Add the shrimp to the skillet and cook for 23 minutes per side until pink and opaque. Remove the shrimp from the skillet and set aside.
3. In the same skillet, add the sliced bell peppers and zucchini. Stirfry for 34 minutes until slightly tender.
4. Return the cooked shrimp to the skillet. Add the lemon juice and lemon zest, and season with salt and pepper.
5. Stir fry for an additional 2 minutes to allow the flavors to meld together.
6. Garnish with fresh parsley and serve hot.

Ginger Soy Chicken And Broccoli Stir Fry

Ingredients:

- 2 tbsps honey
- 1 tbsp grated fresh ginger
- 2 cloves garlic, minced
- 1 tbsp sesame oil
- 4 cups broccoli florets
- 1 red bell pepper, sliced
- 2 green onions, sliced
- 1 lb (450g) boneless, skinless chicken breasts, thinly sliced
- 2 tbsps low sodium soy sauce

- 2 tbsps rice vinegar

- Sesame seeds for garnish

Directions:

1. In a small bowl, whisk together the soy sauce, rice vinegar, honey, grated ginger, and minced garlic.
2. Set aside. Heat the sesame oil in a large skillet or wok over mediumhigh heat. Add the chicken slices and stirfry for 45 minutes until cooked through. Remove the chicken from the skillet and set aside.
3. In the same skillet, add the broccoli florets and sliced red bell pepper. Stirfry for 34 minutes until the vegetables are tendercrisp.
4. Return the cooked chicken to the skillet. Pour the ginger soy sauce over the chicken and

vegetables, and stirfry for an additional 2 minutes to coat everything evenly.
5. Garnish with sliced green onions and sesame seeds before serving.

Spicy Tofu And Mixed Vegetable Stir Fry

Ingredients:

- 1 tbsp olive oil
- 3 cloves garlic, minced
- 1 red bell pepper, sliced
- 1 yellow bell pepper, sliced
- 1 small head broccoli, cut into florets
- 1 cup sugar snap peas
- 1 lb (450g) firm tofu, cubed
- 2 tbsps soy sauce
- 2 tbsps sriracha sauce

- 1 tbsp sesame oil

- 1 tbsp rice vinegar

- 2 tsps cornstarch

- 2 cups cooked brown rice

Directions:

1. In a small bowl, whisk together the soy sauce, sriracha sauce, sesame oil, rice vinegar, and cornstarch to make the sauce. Set aside.
2. Heat the olive oil in a large skillet or wok over medium heat. Add the minced garlic and sauté for 1 minute until fragrant.
3. Add the cubed tofu to the skillet and stirfry for 57 minutes until golden and slightly crispy.
4. Add the sliced bell peppers, broccoli florets, and sugar snap peas to the skillet. Stirfry for

an additional 5 minutes until the vegetables are tendercrisp.
5. Pour the prepared sauce over the tofu and vegetables. Stirfry for 23 minutes until the sauce thickens and coats everything evenly.
6. Serve the spicy tofu and mixed vegetable stirfry over cooked brown rice.

Pumpkin And Lentil Soup.

Ingredients:

- 4 cups vegetable broth
- 1 cup diced carrots
- 1 teaspoon ground cumin
- 1/2 teaspoon ground cinnamon
- 1 cup red lentils
- 1 can (15 ounce) pumpkin puree
- Salt and pepper to taste

Directions:

1. Rinse red lentils and place them in a pot.

2. Add pumpkin puree, vegetable broth, diced carrots, ground cumin, and ground cinnamon to the pot.
3. Simmer until lentils are cooked and vegetables are tender.
4. Add pepper and salt to taste when seasoning.
5. Serve the Pumpkin and Lentil Soup warm for a comforting and nourishing meal.

Cauliflower Rice And Veggie Stirfry.

Ingredients:

- 2 tablespoons soy sauce
- 1 tablespoon vegetable oil
- 1 teaspoon minced garlic
- 1 medium cauliflower, grated or processed into rice like texture
- 2 cups mixed stir fry vegetables (such as bell peppers, carrots, and peas)
- Salt and pepper to taste

Directions:

1. In a pan, heat vegetable oil over medium heat.

2. Add minced garlic and sauté for a minute until fragrant.
3. Add mixed stir fry vegetables and cook until they are slightly tender.
4. Stir in the cauliflower rice and continue to cook until it's heated through.
5. Pour soy sauce over the stirfry and mix well to combine.
6. Add salt and pepper to taste when seasoning.
7. Serve the Cauliflower Rice and Veggie StirFry as a delicious and nutritious meal.

Asparagus Frittata

Ingredients:

- 1 bunch asparagus, trimmed and cut into 1inch pieces
- Salt and freshly ground black pepper
- 8 large eggs
- 1/4 cup grated Parmesan cheese
- 1 tablespoon olive oil
- 2 cloves garlic, minced
- 2 tablespoons chopped fresh parsley

Directions:

1. Preheat oven to 350°F.

2. Heat olive oil in a large ovensafe skillet over medium heat. Add garlic and asparagus and season with salt and pepper. Cook, stirring occasionally, until asparagus is tender, about 5 minutes.
3. In a large bowl, whisk together eggs, Parmesan cheese, and parsley. Pour egg mixture into skillet. Cook, stirring occasionally, until edges begin to set, about 3 minutes.
4. Transfer skillet to preheated oven and bake for 20 minutes, or until frittata is set.
5. Slice and serve.

www.ingramcontent.com/pod-product-compliance
Lightning Source LLC
LaVergne TN
LVHW010226070526
838199LV00062B/4739